ORDER - THEN WAIT

NEVILLE GODDARD

COPYRIGHT INFORMATION

Copyright © 2016 by

IMAGINATIONANDFAITH.COM

All rights reserved. No part of this publication may be reproduced, distributed, or transmitted in any form or by any means, including photocopying, recording, or other electronic or mechanical methods, without the prior written permission of the publisher, except in the case of brief quotations embodied in critical reviews and certain other noncommercial uses permitted by copyright law.

ISBN-13: 978-1546322078
ISBN-10: 1546322078

VISIT OUR WEBSITE

READ AND LISTEN TO HUNDREDS OF NEVILLE'S LECTURES @

WWW.IMAGINATIONANDFAITH.COM

OUR YOUTUBE CHANNEL

https://www.youtube.com/imaginationandfaith

QUOTES

"Chance or accident is not responsible for the things that happen to you, nor is predestined fate the author of your fortune or misfortune. Your subconscious impressions determine the conditions of your world. The subconscious is not selective; it is impersonal and no respecter of persons. The subconscious is not concerned with the truth or falsity of your feeling. It always accepts as true that which you feel to be true. Feeling is the assent of the subconscious to the truth of that which is declared to be true. Because of this quality of the subconscious there is nothing impossible to man. Whatever the mind of man can conceive and feel as true, the subconscious can and must objectify. Your feelings create the pattern from which your world is fashioned, and a change of feeling is a change of pattern." — **Neville Goddard, Resurrection**

"Change your conception of yourself and you will automatically change the world in which you live. Do not try to change people; they are only messengers telling you who you are. Revalue yourself and they will confirm the change." — **Neville Goddard**, **Your Faith is Your Fortune**

"I AM wealthy, poor, healthy, sick, free, confined were first of all impressions or conditions felt before they became visible expressions. Your world is your consciousness objectified. Waste no time trying to change the outside; change the within or the impression; and the without or expression will take care of itself. When the truth of this statement dawns upon you, you will know that you have found the lost word or the key to every door. I AM (your consciousness) is the magical lost word which was made flesh in the likeness of that which you are conscious of being." — **Neville Goddard, Your Faith is Your Fortune**

ORDER – THEN WAIT

God and man are inseparable. We are all members of the Divine Body, partakers of the Divine nature. We cannot be separated. We are one.

Now, let us turn to Scripture for confirmation of what I have just said. I now quote from the 64th chapter of the Book of Isaiah: "O Lord, Thou art our Father. We are the clay. Thou art our Potter. We are the work of Thy hand."

Now, listen to it carefully. The word translated the "Lord" is "I AM." That is our Father; and you can't put "I AM" away from yourself. Now, the word translated "potter" is "imagination." He didn't say, "the potter," – "our Potter."

So, "O Lord, Thou art our Father; we are the clay. Thou art our Potter; we are the work of Thy hand."

So here, my own wonderful human imagination is now identified with the Lord. It's the word "Jehovah." And this is called the "father." So, I am Self-begotten. We are self-begotten. We're not the product of something other than ourselves. These terms are interchangeable!

"the Lord,"

"Father," "Potter," "Imagination." For "potter" is defined in the Concordance as "imagination; that which forms or molds into form; that which makes a resolution; that which determines." For we are told, "Commune with your own hearts on your beds and be silent."

For, "if we know that He hears us in whatever we ask, we know that we have obtained the request from Him."

It's not "another." Can I actually have that confidence in myself? Can I actually, this night, commune with my own heart on my bed and be silent? – knowing that I heard what I did? I know exactly what I did. Can I have confidence in that action? for there is no other god. There is no other "Lord" to whom I can turn.

Let us take, now, the 18th chapter of Jeremiah. He said, "My people have forgotten me and burned incense to false gods." You read that in the 18th chapter, the 15th verse, of Jeremiah.

But now we go back to the beginning of the chapter; "And the word came to Jeremiah from the Lord." The word "Jeremiah" means "Jehovah will rise," which implies in his name that he is asleep and has not yet been awakened. "The word came to Jeremiah from the Lord: Arise and go down to the Potter's house, and I will let you hear my word."

So, "I went down to the Potter's house, and there he was, working at his wheel; but the vessel in his hand was spoiled; so he re-worked it into another vessel, as it seemed good to the potter to do."

We have just discovered that "potter" is my own imagination. I go down to the potter's house. Well, I have just been told "our Potter" is one with the Lord, who is our Father. So, where do I go? Into some little place where a man is working with clay? Oh, he is working with clay, but I've just discovered that I am the clay. "We are the clay." We are the fruit of your efforts; we have discovered Who He is. He is my own imagination! So, I turn to my own imagination, and I wonder, What did you imagine yourself to be today? Broke? Unemployed? Let out? What did you do this day in the Potter's house? for the Potter is your own wonderful human imagination.

Now, this day, what was the concept you held of yourself? It's entirely up to me, for there's no one to whom I can turn. I have to turn to my Self. Well, that is the Potter! And that is the only Jehovah; that's the only Lord, the only Jesus.

So when asked, "What, do you think of Jesus?" Blake replied, "It is the only God; but so am I, and so are you."

"Jesus" is "God-awake." He is the Jeremiah when he sleeps; that is "Jehovah-willarise." He does arise, and when He rises, it is "God-awake."

So, I will go down, – if I know the story, I will still go down while I still am asleep. I am not fully aware of the fact I am the Being spoken of, but I will test it. I will try it. I'll go to the Potter's house; and the Potter is my own imagination.

Now, this day, what did I imagine? Was it spoiled in my hand? Or, was it something that I thought lovely, and I want to preserve it and make it a real state in my world? Or, could I change it somewhat and make it better? Well, if I could make it better, then make it better, because there is no one to whom I can turn. I must go to my own heart on my own bed; and then when I do what I am called upon to do, be silent, – have complete trust in that which I have done.

If I have complete trust in it, it must come to pass because there is no other Creator. There is no Creator in the world but your own wonderful human imagination, and that is the Immortal You.

It cannot cease to be when this little "garment" that you are now "wearing" for creative purposes is taken off, – and you'll do it. You will take it off on time.

Whether the world calls it "suicide" or not, every death is a suicide, because there is no one else to take it from me, even though he shoots me! No matter what he does to me, it's only myself, because we are all "partakers of the one Divine nature." We are all coexistent with God, and God and man are inseparable. They are one.

So, I cannot turn to another, although in my blindness, I burn incense to a false god. I am called upon to be perfectly still and know: I AM GOD. As we are told in the 46th Psalm, the 10th verse:

"Be still and know I am God. I kill; I make alive. I wound; I heal." I do all these things. "And there is none that can deliver out of my hand."

Your 32d chapter of Deuteronomy, your 39th verse – there is no one doing anything but God, and God and man are one; but the Man of Whom I speak is your own wonderful human imagination. That's the real You, the Immortal You.

So, in the Book of Amos, he asks the question: "Does evil befall a city, unless God has done it?" "Does evil befall a city, unless God has done it?"

Now we know Who God is; so all the horrors of the world that befall us, – God did it! But who is God? Our own wonderful human imagination. Yes, even the earthquakes, the volcanoes, – every horror of the world, and every lovely thing in the world, – our own wonderful human imagination did it, because that is one with the Lord Jehovah. There is only one God, and there is no other god.

Now, if you think that it is atheistic, you may think what you will, but I don't think you will. But the world, not yet brought into this concept will think it so. Yet I can tell you, before we began the Fall, – we didn't fall because of some mistake we made. This was a deliberate descent in consciousness to this level for a purpose: to prove our own creative power, that we could actually come down into this world and face death – what seems to be eternal death, and conquer it. Not pretend we are dying, but actually die, and see them all die around us, and still conquer it. But before we came down, we set up a plan. We prepared a way for ourselves to return, and that way is described in Scripture, – and I've told it night after night after night; for no one can really see you – the Real Being that you are. They see the mask that you wear, but not the Being that you are. Not through mortal eyes can they see it.

His Glory is completely hidden from mortal eyes, but you will know it when you see the Son. That Son – the sum total of all the experiences of the world – stands before you, and then you know. Memory returns. And he will stand before everyone in this world, and memory will return; and then comes the final curtain when it comes down on all, and we are the brothers that we were "before that the world was." Everyone glorified, every one returned to the glory that he deliberately, consciously gave up to assume the limitation of these "garments" that we are "wearing" now.

We will not shirk it. All the "garments," all the weaknesses that we took upon ourselves, – I am telling you from experience.

Here, yesterday morning, it's a little after 4:00; and these very wise men – seemingly wise men – in the medical field; and then a woman, an attractive lady in her 40's, and she was a psychiatrist, also of the medical field but a psychiatrist. And I was brought into the picture of the three and they were giving me all this nonsense; and I said, "I know exactly your intention, but to me it's all stupid. It's all nonsense."

Then came into my mind that which I knew I wrote unnumbered years ago, "before that the world was"; it's recorded in Scripture. But memory returns. They were so wise – these grand adults. I said, "Except ye become as a little child, ye cannot enter the Kingdom of Heaven," and they looked startled. I said, "Well now, I am intelligent enough to know what you are telling me.

I understand every word you are telling me, but I do not accept it. Now, a little child may not understand what I am telling the child, but the child trusts me. It has confidence in me, and will say, "I believe."

Unless you, with all your so-called wisdom of this world – the outside, conscious world – can drop it and believe the story that I will tell you, for if I told you what I have experienced, you in your present conscious state could not accept it. You have to turn and become as a child to really accept it. If I told you of a different kind of a birth than that which you know, and the only thing that you know, – and you are giving me all this, – I am giving you the word "baloney," for that's what I meant, – all this nonsense and she came to me and placed her face against mine.

I said, I know exactly what your intentions are. That is your therapy? May I tell you? it's stupid! I have not a thing wrong with me; and secondly, your therapy is nonsense, pure nonsense. If you will only listen for one moment, I will tell you what your reasoning mind cannot accept; but if you will become as a child – for I know from my own experience, – I have a little nephew who came through from Thailand recently, and he came over and I told him a story. He could not understand my story, but I said, "Do you believe that, Roger?"

"Yes!" He believes it. He couldn't understand what I am talking about, but he trusted me; and in trusting me, he believed it.

So, Blake, in writing his friend, Samuel Palmer, said: "You could see what I see, but you do not trust or cultivate it. All you have to do is simply work up imagination to the state of vision, and it's done." The whole thing is done! So, you can see what I see and do what I do, and all you need do is to work up imagination to the state of vision, and the thing is done!

So, he did not claim for himself something apart from Palmer; he was talking to his friend, Samuel Palmer, and thought, Well now, you, are endowed with a certain faculty. He said, "I, too, have the faculty, but I cultivate it. I have the faculty and you have the faculty because we are one. Jesus, – yes, is the only God, but so am I and so are you."

Jesus is God-awake; and I am telling you from experience, he sleeps in all. Call him "Father," call him "Joseph," who sleeps. He is the Dreamer. When he awakes, he is Jesus; and Jesus who calls himself the Son is one with the Father, but now the Father is awake, for in the end there is only God. There is only the Father.

So, I tell you, your own wonderful human imagination is God! It's not like God; it is God! There is no other god. And you cannot separate it, not for one moment. If you do, you'll burn incense to false gods and you will make all kinds of things on the outside of yourself and worship it; and that is not God.

I am speaking of the Immortal You that cannot die. It cannot die! That is God, – so confident that it could overcome death that it gave up its beauty, its glorified Body, and took upon itself this [indicating the physical body] and became obedient unto death, even death upon this "cross." And yet, it could overcome it.

But I tell you, not one is going to fail. Many will doubt it, but not one can fail! He would leave the ninety and nine, who awoke, and go in search of the one who is still asleep. I cannot for one moment rest if one of my brothers is not redeemed. And may I tell you? the world may not believe this, may not know it; but it is the true and reawakening of imagination that the whole vast world aches for. That is a spiritual experience that crowns and redeems experience. It is that great event that actually crowns this experience, for without that, what would be the experience?

It is the awakening of the Being Who deliberately fell asleep to have this experience, because this power is so great, unless, he gave up his power and his glorified body, what challenge could you give him? So, he had to completely give it up, and take upon himself the restrictions and the limitations of man– this little thing here [indicating the body].

But That Which is now dreaming in man is one with God, and is God. That is the Father. So, "O Lord, Thou art our Father; we are the clay. Thou art our Potter, and we are the work of Thy hand." Our imagination is the Lord. Our imagination is the Father, and in search of the Father.

I am in search of mySelf. I am looking for mySelf; and when I find Him, I find Him only through the means that I set up in the beginning "before that the world was," and that was a son. For if I am a father, there must be a son. So, I set him up in the beginning, that when I go through all the experiences that I can ever have in the world of death and decay, – when I come out of it, it has to mold itself into one being, and that is the fruit of my effort, and he is the son, and his name is David.

So, when I meet David, suddenly the whole thing returns, and here is my memory. That which I gave up returns, and he stands before me, and he calls me, Father. I am his lord; I am his father; and I know I am, and he knows I am; and that is the Crown that redeems the experiences, the horrors that I have gone through. For I have played all the parts. Not one part could I have omitted. Yes, the thief and the judge, the murderer and the murdered; I have played every part in the world. And that is why today, I can actually say, "Father," – meaning mySelf, – "forgive them, for they do not know in their state of sleep what they do." Leave them just as they are. But tell the story over and over. "How often, Lord?"

"Seventy times seven."

Keep on telling it and telling it until it gets through and starts to shake the Dreamer within the one who is listening to you.

So, "unless you turn," said he, "and become as a child, you cannot enter the Kingdom of Heaven." So, all the educations of men, all these wonderful honors that we have applied on each other, – they bury the mind and stop it from actually becoming like the child.

What I am telling you I could never have discovered through reason. I never could have found it in a book. It is in the Bible, but I didn't see it until it happened. Now I share with you what is already in the Bible, but I didn't know it until I experienced it. And when I experienced it, I began to really search Scripture to find that it was always there!

When I read that chapter, little did I realize that, "Thou, Lord, art our Father, our Potter." I always thought it meant something on the outside. And then I searched and searched to find that "potter" means "imagination; to mold into a form." But the word is "our Potter," not the imagination, – our imagination. "Thou art our Potter." You mean the Lord? and the word is "Jehovah." They sound it as "Adonai"; "Adonai" is what we use instead of saying Jehovah. All right, so it is called "the Lord," defined in Scripture as "the Self Existent, eternal One, that has no beginning and no end." That is the God, the only Lord; and he is Father.

But it is "our Father." "O Lord, Thou art our Father." And now our Father is our Potter. And I have discovered, our "Potter" is our imagination! So, I am my own Father! But I didn't know it. And how would I know that that Father is the father of David, for David said, "I will tell of the decree of the Lord, and he said unto me, Thou art my son. Today I have begotten thee." But who would have thought for one moment, reading that story, – thousands of years before this moment in time – that it is speaking of me? Speaking of you? That we are the Father who said to David, "Thou art my son."

Then comes the deep, deep dream; and we dream these horrors of the world. And then comes that moment in time when I call myself from the Deep, for I am the Father. I am the Lord; and so, I call my own Being. I awaken myself, as I had predetermined at a certain moment in time after I have played all the parts.

But, "How long, how vast, how severe the anguish 'ere I found my Self were long to tell." But I found my Self, and the only one who could have revealed me to myself was my Son that I set up in the beginning "before that the world was."

So, then we are told: "No one knows who the Son is, except the Father; and no one knows who the Father is, except the Son, and anyone to whom the Son chooses to reveal Him," for he has to reveal Him in the end, and then the Father awakes.

Now, you take that 78th chapter of Psalms. The title of it is Asaph. That is, the Psalm is a Psalm of Asaph. "Asaph" means to gather together and to record, to take all the things and put them together. And then he said, "I will open up my mouth in a parable and utter dark sayings from of old," – dark sayings from of old, things that are difficult and hard to understand. Then, now, he goes through the entire story of Israel, as we call it in the Old Testament, and he tells the entire story, and he tells you it is a parable. He tells you they are dark sayings, hard to understand; and then he comes to the end – it is a nice long chapter, – and what does he say? "And the Lord awoke as from sleep, like a man rising out of strong drink." And then he declared David. David is his Prince. David is his Shepherd over all the people.

At the very end, he records all the things through which man has gone, and then comes: "The Lord begins to awake," and He awakes as one out of sleep, like one waking from wine, strong wine, – as though it were a drunken sleep, where all things could happen; and then He awakes! And who does he call? He calls David. And the whole thing ends on the note of David, after the entire series of parables.

So, a parable is a story told as though it were true, letting the one who hears it wrestle with it, letting him discover the meaning behind the written word. It's told as though it were true. Now, one has to discover the fiction from the fact. What is it trying to convey? It is telling a story. You will pass through the Red Sea. You will lift up the serpent in the wilderness. He is telling all these stories; and then it comes: "And then the Lord awakes."

He awakes from the parable, and finds the kernel. He finds the truth; and then He calls David. So David comes into view, and David stands before you and calls you, Father. And the joy that comes upon you when you see your son standing before you, – you have no other child, just David. For your child in this world is a brother.

I have a son, I have a daughter; they are both my "brothers" in Eternity. I have a wife, and I have other brothers here; they are all my "brothers" in Eternity. For in Eternity, we are all above the organization of sex. We are the Elohim; and the "Elohim" is a plural words "one made up of others," – Elohim.

So, all of us are the gods who came down. So, when you hear the word tomorrow or you think of it tonight, do not let the mind jump to something on the outside. "Commune with your own heart upon your bed, and then be silent." But see that you commune as you want to mold that picture, for the whole verse is this: "Be angry, but sin not. Commune with your own heart upon your bed, and be silent."

But it doesn't tell you not to be angry. So, the day has been an explosive day – explode! Be angry, "but sin not." To "sin" is to "miss the mark." Don't now go to bed and let the sun descend upon your anger. All right, – explode! Get it off your chest, as it were. Now take the whole thing that you would throw away in the past as a broken vessel and you can't repair it. No; keep the same vessel, and rework it now into a new shape as it seems good to you to do.

So, the end of a day, – all right, so it wasn't a good day. Explode, and then; "But sin not. Don't let the sun descend upon your anger." Stand right there, and simply rework it. Rework what being? Rework yourself! You are the clay. This thing here [indicating the physical man) is seeing the world based upon what you have assumed that you are. So, now you actually do it.

Now, let me share with you a story. The lady is here tonight, – this is the mother. She said, "Our son kept talking and talking and talking that he wanted a mini-bike. Well, his father and I did not want him to have a mini-bike; but he kept on talking and talking and talking about it; so, one day I thought, Now I will show him. I said, 'Now tell me, Dusty, if you had your mini-bike, where would it be now?' He said, 'In the garage.'"

She said, "All right, it's now in the garage. Right? There it is. Now, will you go and get it, and where would you use it?"

"Well," he said, "I would use it in the driveway."

Well, the mother said to Dusty, "Well, you can't do that, for we have neighbors, and they have stated in no uncertain terms they will not tolerate a mini-bike on their driveway; and their driveway joins ours. So, they will not allow it. Now, where else would you use it?"
"Well, I would use it on the street. I would drive it on the street."

"But is that allowed?" the mother said.

"Well," he said, "I don't know."

"Well, go and call the police and find out."

So, he went to the 'phone and called the police, and the police said, "No, you are not allowed to use a mini-bike on the streets."

All right, that was that. "Now, where else would you use it?"

"Well, in the May lot. The May Company has a huge big parking lot; I'll go over there and use it."

"You have to have permission. All right, go and call the May Company and ask for permission." So, he went to the 'phone and called the May Company; and they said, "No; we are open seven days a week, and so we cannot allow a mini-bike in our parking lot for we have it used by our customers seven days a week."

So, when he got that, he went to his room for half an hour; and when he came out, he said, "I have made a decision. I don't really want a mini-bike at all."

And then the mother said, "You know, how often I've done the same thing! I thought really I wanted this – I really want this, and then I ask myself, Now what would I do with it after I got it?
Now, I have it now; what am I going to do with it? And I discovered, you know, I really don't want it at all!"

Well, may I tell you? having lived in one apartment in New York City for fourteen years – the last apartment we had before we moved out here, we lived almost fourteen years in that apartment. It was a seven-room apartment – a duplex. I had no idea what junk we stored over fourteen years! We called in our Sisters-in-Law, that is, Bill's two sisters, and her aunt and said, 'Pick out all these things.' They took one third of our furniture, and said, 'There it is, take what you can.'"

What they didn't take, we called the church and said, "Send your van for it for your thrift shop." We gave away a third of what we had accumulated. When we came out here, I regretted I hadn't given away fifty per cent or maybe two-thirds. When we came out here, I couldn't find places for my books. I gave away over four hundred books that I felt I didn't need. I had read them; that was part of my growth.

As a man grows in this world, he is growing from a god of tradition into a God of experience; so, these were part of my growth in the god of tradition. And then I still kept them. Well, maybe someone can use them now; so I gave a friend of mine who lives here, well over four hundred books, and I gave another fifty or so books – and all these; and I still have too many books!
You grow, and you outgrow, and you grow and you outgrow; and all these things that we kept and kept and kept for fourteen years, we accumulated them. Where we kept them, I really do not know: under the bed, under this, – all places. And finally came the day of moving.

That's why, not to burden my wife, I hope I go first, that she will have the pleasure of weeding out what we have now, because I couldn't face it, really – the thought of all that you accumulate.

We have been here now ten years in the present apartment. And knowing what happened after fourteen years, I despair when I think of what eventually must take place when we do move, as we all have to move in this world.

So, the mother is perfectly right, now, in taking that little lesson, which she had learned before. I want so-and-so; but if I really had it, then where would it be now? Then she comes to the conclusion, I really don't want it at all.

They must have it. I have a Sister-in-Law, – she's now a widow, for my brother Lawrence died. She always must have the biggest of everything in the family. My sister, who could well afford anything in this world, for she really is the richest of all because all her brothers see to it that she keeps everything that she ever made, and they invest it for her, – but she has a lovely string of pearls. No! this Sister-in- Law had to have a bigger string of pearls, something fantastic. Well, it came now to little diamond earrings. She had to have the biggest thing in the world.

She wouldn't go to her own husband to pierce her ears. She wanted them pierced so she could carry these big things in her ears. So she went to her brother, who also was a doctor; and he unfortunately made the hole too low. These things are so big that they will pull her down to here [indicating]. Now, they cannot be the world's best diamonds, because you can't have diamonds that big and only pay $8,000 for them. For the two rings cost $8,000. Well, you can't have an eight-thousand-dollar diamond that big and be a good diamond. She doesn't know that; so now she can't wear them. Where are they? In a safe. But she had to have the biggest thing in the world. Had she only known this story that my friend knows tonight, – if I had them, where would they be? On my ears? Yes; that is why I bought them. Would they be comfortable? She never thought of that. She never thought of this enormous thing pulling on her lobe, and so she has the two rocks. What good are they? Were I she, I'd give them away, – give them to anyone who wants to have this nonsense. But, no; she can't part with anything. That, I do know. Now, she is traveling the world over, and all of her things are in storage in Barbados. More silver than you would need to open any silver shop. More sets of dishes than you would need to feed a hundred without borrowing a dish. She had to have more and more.

So, that is what one gets without thinking: If I had it, what would I do with it? I will tell you a simple, simply technique. Set your whole mind on what I have been telling you from night to night on the Grace that is coming to you, which means that you are going to awake! When you awake, you own the world! You don't have a little cottage. The world is yours, for the world is God's; and you are God when you awake. The whole vast universe is the Lord's, and you are the Lord. You cannot separate the Reality that is man from the Creator of the universe. You are one. "So, set your hope fully on that grace that is coming to you at the unveiling of Jesus Christ within you," for Jesus Christ is God-awake.

So, when He awakes, He awakes in you as you; not as "another." Then the whole vast world is yours, and you see it through entirely different eyes. You see everything differently, – a beauty that no one, looking only through mortal eyes, could ever conceive.

So, when you go home, try to remember what I've told you; and when you read Scripture, it's all about you! So, when you read, "O Lord, Thou art our Father; we are the clay. Thou art our Potter; we are the work of Thy hands," remember these three are interchangeable terms: my "imagination," the "Father," and the "Lord" are interchangeable terms. And now I'll go down to the Potter, for the Potter, I've just discovered, is my own imagination. I will stand still and now, in my own imagination, watch: What did I this day do? What did I imagine? And now if what I imagined this day is spoiled, is not what I want to make real in my world, – don't discard it. Rework it into another vessel, as it seems good to you to do.

You can't discard any one; just rework it into an entirely different vessel as it seems good to you to do. And if one will not accept it, pass along. It's perfectly all right. Eventually they will awake; and when they awake, they are our brother.

And we will wait for Eternity, if it takes Eternity, for everyone to come back, for we are incomplete if one is missing. And one cannot be missing, for the Lord is made up of all of us. He has no being without us. We are members of the Divine Body, all of us; and we share in that Divine nature, – the same Creative Power. And may I tell you? when you are clothed in that "garment" which you gave up, wherever you go, it is perfect, automatically perfect. You don't have to raise a finger to make it so. It is perfect, because you are clothed in your Glorified Body.
So, tonight you dwell upon what you really are, and don't turn to the left or the right. Don't burn incense to any false god. "Commune with your own heart upon your bed, and then be silent."

What would it be like if it were true? Can you answer that? If you can answer that, then what was said in that First Epistle of John, the 5th chapter, the 15th verse: "If we know that he hears us in whatever we ask, we know that we have obtained the request made of him."

What a Promise! "If we know He hears," – well, don't I know what I've heard? Don't I know what I've just done? All right; that is the One spoken of.

Well, can I really believe what I have just imagined? Can I? Well then, I must know, now, if I am putting my trust in This One, which is my own imagination, – well then, I will know I have obtained it. It has already been done. Now wait for it. It's done!

Like a shipment. I have complete confidence in a shipment coming if I have ordered it; so you order, and then you wait! It may come by slow freight, it may come by express, it may come by air freight; it'll come. The vision is maturing; "and if it seems long, then wait, for it is sure, and it will not be late." [Habakkuk 2:3]

THE END.

Made in the USA
Monee, IL
15 February 2025